The Vanishing

The Renee MacRae Case

Murder World

Scotland

Book 3

D1586023

Murder World: Real crimes, real killers.

Table of Contents

Introduction

Colm MacGregor peered tiredly into the darkness ahead. The journey from Glasgow had taken three hours so far and driving the bus through the darkness of a bitterly cold November Friday night was hard work. But now, he was only twelve miles or so from his destination, the city of Inverness. There was relatively little traffic on the normally busy A9 at this time in the evening and the darkness ahead was almost total, broken only by the occasional, isolated lights of a small farm in the distance or a passing car. This is one of the most remote and desolate parts of Britain and it was always a relief to crest the last small hill and begin the long descent into Inverness.

However, before he got to that point, at about nine o'clock in the evening, Colm MacGregor saw something odd up ahead in the distance. As he got closer, he realized that he could see something burning, not far from the road. He slowed up and tried to understand what he was looking at. Something was certainly on fire – he could see flames reaching up into the dark night sky. But, whatever it was seemed to be hidden behind a low embankment close to the road. When it was less than one hundred yards ahead, he could see that whatever was burning was in a lay-by next to the road. There were no passengers on the bus, so he swung in to see if anyone needed help. As he drew close, he could see a car burning up ahead. He stopped the bus and got out. Even standing thirty feet away, he could feel the intense heat from the fire.

The whole interior of the car was on fire. He shielded his eyes, but it was difficult to see if there was anyone inside. He didn't think so, but the smoke and flames made it impossible to be certain. But then it was also odd that there wasn't anyone there. If someone had realized that their car was on fire and had pulled into the lay-by, they should still have been in the vicinity – it was obvious that the car hadn't been burning for long. But there was no-one else to be seen.

Knowing that he couldn't help if there was anyone inside the car and worried that the fuel tank might explode, Colm MacGregor got back into his bus and drove to the nearest farm where he used the telephone to summon the Fire Brigade and police. He couldn't have guessed that this would start the longest missing person enquiry Scotland has ever seen nor that it would mark the beginning of a bizarre and unsettling investigation into the disappearance of the two people last seen in the car – a thirty-six year old woman and her three year old son.

This is the story of the forty year search to discover what happened to Renee and Andrew MacRae on that dark, November evening in 1976.

Due to their actions or the circumstances in which they find themselves, the names of certain people enter the lexicon of popular understanding and become widely used synonyms. In the UK for example, the term *'doing a Lord Lucan'* became widely used to describe a person who disappeared in mysterious circumstances after the titular Lord went off the radar after apparently murdering his maid in 1974. However, in Scotland in the seventies and eighties, another name began to be used to characterize a mysterious disappearance: *'Renee MacRae'*.

One November evening in 1976, thirty-six year old Renee MacRae and her three year old son Andrew vanished completely and seemingly forever from a lonely road in the Highlands of Scotland. The case sparked massive media interest and intense speculation. What had happened to Renee and Andrew and where were they?

Although it was widely covered in the national press at the time, the case of Renee MacRae is less well-known now. Perhaps that is because people like their crime stories to be neatly completed with a solution, a trial and a conviction? In general we like to know who is innocent, who is guilty and why the crime happened. The Renee MacRae case lacks such closure and it seems unlikely that there will ever be a trial and a conviction (this is now officially the UK's longest running missing person investigation). However, the fact that, forty years on, we still don't know what happened is also what makes this case fascinating. This is one of the most enduring mysteries in the annals of Scottish crime. Just what did befall Renee and Andrew MacRae? Are they really dead? If so, what happened to them and where are their bodies?

With the benefit of hindsight and the application of logic and little bit of common sense, I think it is still possible to look at this fascinating case in a fresh way.

Prologue

The city of Inverness likes to call itself '*The Gateway to the Highlands*' and, for the hundreds of thousands of tourists who visit each year, that's precisely what it is: a place they pass through on their way to somewhere else. The Highlands of Scotland officially begins north of the Great Glen – the huge fault line which includes Lochs Ness, Lochy and Linnie and bisects Scotland from east to west. Everything south of the Great Glen is classed as Lowlands and everything to the north is the Highlands and Inverness neatly straddles the divide between the two.

Looking east along the Great Glen and Loch Ness towards Inverness.

Photo: David Broad

In summer, tourists provide a noisy backdrop to days that seem to last forever. Many people forget that Inverness is in the far north, further north than Moscow in Russia and Malmo in Sweden and almost as close to the Arctic Circle as it is to London. At the height of summer, it never really gets dark here at all – the sun doesn't set until nine thirty in the evening and rises again at three o'clock in the morning and the period between is never darker than a milky grey twilight.

The downside to the endless days of summer is that from November to February, when the hordes of tourists vanish, the locals endure a winter that is as bitter and dark as can be found almost anywhere on the planet. In the middle of winter, the sun doesn't rise in Inverness until nine in the morning and it sets again at three thirty in the afternoon. Not that you're likely to see much sun here in the winter – the murky skies mean that it's possible to go for days or sometimes weeks without seeing anything more dramatic than a slight lightening of the sky during the alleged hours of daylight. Inverness in winter is not a place for anyone who is prone to depression.

The landscape is also a factor. It can be beautiful, but large parts of it are also bleak and inhospitable. There is a great deal of empty countryside in this part of the world – in parts of the Highlands there are fewer than two people for every square kilometer of land, and that is an average which includes cities. In contrast, for example, the average figure for the whole of England is over four hundred people for every square kilometer of land and in Greater London that rises to over one thousand-five hundred people for every square kilometer. There are parts of the highlands where it is possible to look to the horizon and not be able to see a single habitation, road or building of any sort. This is immediately evident if you choose to drive south from the city of Inverness.

The A9 south of Inverness

Photo: Mick Knapton

The A9, the main road linking Inverness with Perth in the South and Wick in the north, is the longest road in Scotland and it meanders through mountain passes and high valleys on its journey from Falkirk in the south to Scrabster Harbour in Thurso in the north. Following the A9 south from Inverness, the first thing you'll notice is that you climb rapidly, leaving Inverness and the Moray Firth behind as the road heads towards Slochd Summit, 1,328 feet above the sea, but just seventeen miles from Inverness. Not long after leaving Inverness the A9 travels through the hills round Daviot and Moy and even here, just a few miles from the city centre, the landscape is bleak in the winter. It's a forbidding and lonely place where it would be very easy for a fanciful person to imagine bad things happening. A breakdown. An accident. Perhaps even a murder...

Chapter 1: Beginnings

Christina Catherine MacDonald was born at Raigmore hospital in Inverness in 1940, just as the Battle of Britain was nearing its height over London and the fields of Sussex. The war came to Scotland too – there were over five hundred German bombing raids on Scottish targets in the early years of the war and there were large numbers of civilian casualties in the worst affected targets in Aberdeen, Edinburgh and Glasgow. In Inverness though, there was limited enemy activity and in Beauly, the small market town ten miles to the north where Christina's family lived in a council house, the war had little direct impact.

It is a common practice in the Highlands (though one that frequently baffles outsiders) that people have both a formal, given name and a different name by which they are known to friends and family. In Christina's case, she was known to almost everyone as '*Reenie*' which, over the years, became the rather more sophisticated sounding '*Renee*'. Renee was a lively, inquisitive and intelligent girl who was also vivacious and attractive. Although she was bright, she didn't do especially well at school – she was a fun-loving girl who would rather spend time rehearsing the Highland dancing she loved rather than studying for her lessons.

In 1960, she had left school and found a job working at Boots the Chemist in the centre of Inverness. The shop was located on the corner of Inglis Street and the High Street and in 1960 the first floor of the building was occupied by the Boots Lending Library Service. Largely forgotten now, the Boots Lending Library was started in 1898 and by the early 1960s it was one of the most popular library services in the country, providing subscribers with a *'Pay-as-you-read'* option. The Boots library remained popular until the 1964 Public Libraries and Museums Act required local authorities to provide free public lending libraries. In the early 1960s and partly because of the presence of the library, the Boots shop in the centre of Inverness was always busy and the friendly and attractive young woman who worked behind the counter became well-known to many customers.

Boots the Chemist in the centre of Inverness. The lending library was on the first floor, above the pharmacy.

Photo: T. Kenneth MacKenzie, The Highland Council Planning Department

One of those customers was Gordon MacRae, one of twin sons of the wealthy and influential MacRae family. Gordon was just three years older than Rene, handsome, charming, well-dressed and not short of cash. He was immediately smitten with Renee, she was impressed by him and the two began to date.

The MacRae family traced their wealth back to Roderick MacRae, born in 1825 in Strathconon. Like many of his contemporaries, Roderick was brought up to speak Gaelic but learned to speak, read and write English at school in

Strathconon. In 1837, his family was ejected from their house when the owner of the land decided that he wanted to create a deer forest. The twelve year old Roderick was sent to work for an elderly woman, Mrs Matheson at Hedgefield, just outside Beauly. Unknown to the boy, his employer deducted one pound from his wages every week and invested this money in a bank account set up in his name. To this she added two pounds of her own money every week until her death at which time Roderick discovered to his great surprise that he was suddenly one of the wealthiest men in the area.

He used the money to buy the Lovat Arms Hotel in Beauly and then, in 1878 and in partnership with another local man, William Dick, he formed a partnership to operate stables and a service where customers could hire a horse and buggy. When horse-drawn transport began to be replaced by motor vehicles in the early 1900s, MacRae & Dick became a dealer in motor cars and rapidly became the largest vehicle retailer in the north of Scotland. In 1933 the MacRae family was a major investor in Highland Airways, the first airline to operate regular passenger services out of Inverness airport. By the early 1960s the MacRae family had interests in a number of local businesses.

After a short courtship, Gordon MacRae and Renee MacDonald were married in 1963 in a high-profile wedding in Inverness. They soon settled into the marriage and to enjoying the kind of lifestyle enjoyed only by those with access to substantial wealth. They moved into a large house in Drummond Crescent, an exclusive development close the beautiful Ness Islands in Inverness. Italy and the Mediterranean became their favourite holiday destinations and the couple escaped there as often as possible. The MacRaes were true jet-setters at a time when, for most people in the Highlands, a foreign holiday meant taking the family to Butlins at Skegness for a week.

Gordon was kept very busy looking after family business interests and in June 1965 the MacRae family launched a new venture: Hugh MacRae & Company (Builders) Limited. There was a sense of optimism about Inverness and its potential for growth and the formation of the new company coincided with the establishment of the Highlands and Islands Development Board (HIDB). The HIDB first met in November 1965 under the Chairmanship of Professor Robert Grieve, one of Scotland's leading planners. The stated function of the board was to *"prepare, concert, promote, assist and undertake measures for the economic and social development of the Highlands and Islands."*

It didn't take long for the Board to find potential projects: members of the Board were involved in sponsoring and supporting research into salmon farming and the possible establishment of a Marine Farming Unit at Ardnamurchan. Board members also met with the Minister for Technology to discuss plans to site a prototype nuclear power station at Dounreay in Sutherland and with Occidental Petroleum in Los Angeles to discuss the building of a petrochemical complex at Invergordon. It's a testament to the commitment and energy of Board members that all these projects subsequently went ahead. So, when in 1965 the Board published its vision for the next twenty years and this included the potential for major development in the Inverness and the Inner Moray Firth Area, no-one doubted that this would happen.

The one common feature of almost all the projects which the HIDB was keen to support was the need for large-scale construction work. It didn't take a huge amount of imagination to realise that these projects would also bring many more people to live in Inverness and surrounding areas and that these incomers would require homes. Starting a construction company in Inverness in 1965 was a very shrewd move and it didn't take long to for this to begin to pay off for the MacRae family.

Gordon MacRae and his twin brother Charles were made directors of the new construction company. Both of them spent a great deal of time making sure that it was profitable and they succeeded, probably beyond their or anyone else's expectations. By the early seventies, Hugh MacRae & Company was turning over hundreds of thousands of pounds each year and it wouldn't take long for this to grow into millions. Gordon MacRae also became personally very wealthy as a result - during the same period he was reputed to have become a millionaire.

Despite Gordon's engagement with the new business and a very high workload, he and Renee appeared to continue to be very happy together. Perhaps there wasn't quite as much time as there had been for foreign holidays, but still, Renee and Gordon lived the kind of life that most people in the Highlands could only dream about. The only thing that was a little surprising to many people was that they didn't have any children. Then, in 1968, Renee gave birth to a boy, Gordon, and it seemed that the couple's happiness was complete.

Chapter 2: One night in November

The success of the building company continued into the early 1970s. Work remained plentiful as Inverness continued to grow and new commercial and industrial projects proliferated. By the mid-seventies, Hugh MacRae & Company (Builders) Limited was reputed to be turning over millions of pounds each year. In 1973, Renee MacRae provided her husband with a second son, Andrew David. However, people who knew the couple well noted that they didn't seem to be getting on quite as well as they had in the past. Renee in particular seemed to have fallen out of love with her husband. Some people initially put this down to a case of postnatal depression after the birth of Andrew but those who knew her well sensed a fundamental and unexplained change in Renee's attitude towards her husband.

Renee MacRae

By early 1974, things had deteriorated to the point that it was generally known that, although Renee and Gordon continued to live together in the same house in Drummond Crescent, they no longer shared a bed and were effectively leading their own lives. Later in 1974, they agreed to formally separate. Renee explained to her husband that she had met another man, though she refused to identify him. She wanted to move out of the shared home and take both children with her. Gordon MacRae seemed to accept the split with remarkable calm. He bought his wife a luxury bungalow in a new development in Cradlehall, east of Inverness and a short distance from Culloden and the A9, and the couple formally separated when she moved out of Drummond Crescent in late 1974.

The two appeared to remain friendly – even after the split Gordon MacRae described Renee as *"a good friend and a wonderful person."* Although Renee was the main carer for the children, she often dropped the boys off to spend time with their father. To ensure that she always had access to reliable transport, Gordon also provided Renee with a car – a BMW 2002, one of the finest family saloon cars available in the mid-1970s. The car was actually owned by Hugh MacRae & Company, but this simply meant that things like servicing, repairs and insurance were all paid for by the company while Renee had exclusive use of the car. Gordon also provided Renee with sufficient money that she was able to continue to lead a very comfortable life – she was able to afford, for example, a housekeeper to look after her new home in Cradlehall.

By late 1976, Gordon and Renee MacRae were both well established in their separate lives. Gordon had become involved with another woman, Vivienne, a former receptionist at Hugh MacRae & Company, though he continued to be on friendly terms with his estranged wife. Although both Gordon and Renee appeared to accept that the marriage was over, neither seemed in a hurry to formalize the situation with a divorce.

1976 was a time of change not just for the MacRaes but for the UK as a whole. The summer of 1976 was one of the hottest on record, reaching almost 100°F in parts of the country and bringing a drought which caused restrictions on the use of water. John Curry became the first Briton to win a gold medal for figure skating at the Winter Olympics and James Hunt became Formula 1 World Champion after a season-long tussle with his rival Nikki Lauda. Harold Wilson resigned as Prime Minister and was replaced by James Callaghan. Much-loved television series *Dixon of Dock Green* finally came to an end in 1976, but popular new shows included *Rentaghost, Multi-Coloured Swap Shop* and *The Fall and Rise of Reginald Perrin*. In October a band called The Damned released the very first single marketed as '*punk rock*' and the Sex Pistols turned a brief appearance on the Bill Grundy television show into notoriety that helped propel their debut single, *Anarchy in the UK*, into the charts. It was a bad year for novelist Agatha Christie and actors Sid James and Alastair Sim – they all died in 1976 but it was a better time for Benedict Cumberbatch and Martine McCutcheon who were both born in this year.

In Inverness, the new Eden Court Theatre opened in April 1976 to provide the first large theatre and arts venue in the Highlands. Construction work began on what would become the Kessock Bridge, a suspension bridge linking Inverness with North Kessock on the Black Isle. The Prototype Fast Reactor at Dounreay in Caithness began providing electricity to the Scottish grid and work continued on upgrading the A9 between Perth and Inverness – there had been so many fatalities on this road in previous years that it had become known as the '*killer A9*' in the press. Inverness had also suffered during the heatwave during the summer – snowploughs had been deployed in July and August to spread sand on Highland roads where the tarmac was actually melting. When the heat of that summer finally ended Inverness, like many parts of the UK, experienced one of the wettest autumns since records began with widespread flooding. By November, the rain had finally eased and the weather was cold but generally dry.

On the morning of November 12th 1976, Renee MacRae dropped her eldest son at school at around 08:50 am before going to have coffee at the house of her closest friend, Valerie Steventon in Cawdor, not far from Cradlehall. She took her housekeeper, Margaret Ross, and her younger son, Andrew, with her. The two women left Ms Steventon's house at around 11:45 and Renee MacRae dropped Mrs Ross back at the house in Cradlehall to do the housework. At 15:00 Renee collected Gordon from school. The sun set at four o'clock that day and by the time that Renee arrived at her husband's office to drop Gordon off at around five o'clock, it was completely dark. She was planning, she told her estranged husband, to spend the weekend with her married sister Morag at her home in Kilmarnock and she would be taking Andrew with her. She would be back, she explained, in time to take her eldest son to school on Monday morning. Renee was wearing a three-quarter length sheepskin coat and brown, knee-length boots over maroon slacks and a dark blue chunky sweater. She left the office and drove off with Andrew in her blue BMW. That was the last known sighting of Renee and Andrew.

The two litre BMW 2002 driven by Renee MacRae was acknowledged as being one of the finest family saloon cars available in 1976.

Photo: nakhon100

At around nine o'clock that evening, a bus driver, Colm MacGregor, was driving his bus north, towards Inverness on the A9. Around twelve miles south of the city and close to Loch Moy, he saw that something was burning in the darkness up ahead. As he got closer, he could see that whatever was in flames was in a lay-by and behind an embankment close to the road. There were no passengers on the bus, so he decided to pull in to lay-by to see what was burning. Most lay-bys on the A9 are simply wider stretches of the road where cars and other vehicles may park adjacent to main carriageway but this one, lay-by 162, is a little different. It is a small loop-road and to access it from the northbound route, a driver must turn off the A9 and follow a narrow track that curves round behind an embankment covered with trees for more than 100 metres. The embankment and trees completely screen any vehicle in the lay-by from sight from the road. When Colm MacGregor pulled his bus into the lay-by he realized that the flames he had seen were coming from a burning blue car in the lay-by. He quickly looked inside, but could see no-one in the car or nearby.

At almost the same time, passengers on a train heading from Glasgow to Inverness also saw the blazing car. The railway line passes only a few yards from the lay-by, on an embankment above it, giving people on the train a very clear view of the burning vehicle in the lay-by below them. The fire must have been rather frightening to see – this is an area almost completely devoid of houses (apart from Dalmagarry Farm on the opposite side of the A9) and comprising mainly open moorland. In the darkness of that November evening, the blaze must have been visible for quite some distance to the south of the A9.

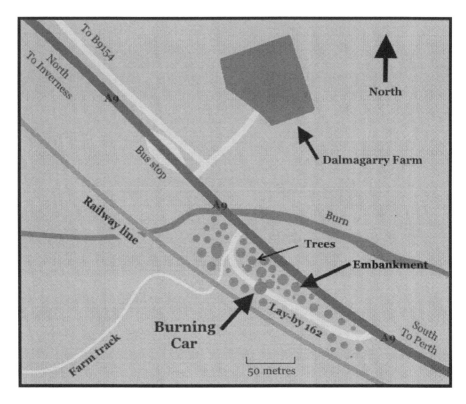

Map showing the location of the burning car and the configuration of lay-by 162.

Colm MacGregor raced to find a telephone and the police and the Fire Service were summoned. There was little that either could do. The car was well ablaze when it was first discovered and by the time that fire-fighting equipment arrived at around ten o'clock, it was almost completely burned-out. It was clear that there was no-one in the car and initially, police assumed that this was a case of a stolen vehicle being burned after being used for joy-riding. Sadly, this was as common in Inverness as it was in other British cities, though the location for the dumping of the vehicle was unusual – stolen cars were more commonly dumped and burned (to remove possible forensic and fingerprint evidence) much closer to the city.

The A9, looking south. This picture is taken just north of the entrance to Dalmagarry Farm. Lay-by 162 is in the trees on the right side of the road (the entrance to the lay-by is arrowed) and the railway embankment is above and behind.

Photo: Dave Fergusson

Police quickly identified the vehicle as a BMW 2002 belonging to Hugh MacRae & Company. They were able to speak with Gordon MacRae who told them that the car was being used by his wife who was in Kilmarnock for the weekend. There was an immediate suspicion that the car might have been stolen out of the railway station car park or some other location after being left there by Mrs MacRae. However, when they were able to contact her married sister, Morag Govans in Kilmarnock, police were surprised to discover that Renee not only wasn't there, her sister hadn't expected to see her that weekend. Morag Govans didn't appear to know where her sister might be and no-one else seemed to know where Renee was.

When Renee MacRae failed to turn up on Monday 15th November to collect her son Gordon as arranged, people began to get very concerned indeed. This concern was increased when police revealed that, inside the boot of the burned-out BMW (almost the only part of the car not completely destroyed by the fire) they had found a blanket. On the blanket was a small amount of what appeared to be blood.

Renee MacRae's burned-out BMW after it had been taken to Northern Constabulary headquarters in Inverness.

Photo: Northern Constabulary

On Monday 15th November officers of Northern Constabulary began a missing person enquiry intended to locate Renee MacRae and her son Andrew. No-one could have guessed that the enquiry would still be active more than forty years later and would eventually become the UK's longest running missing person case.

Chapter 3: Undercurrents

One of the first important facts uncovered by the missing person enquiry was that Renee MacRae had never intended to visit her sister in Kilmarnock over the weekend of 13th/14th November. Valerie Steventon, the friend with who Renee had coffee on the morning of the 12th, explained to police that Renee was actually planning to spend the weekend in Perth with her lover. Ms Steventon also explained that Renee's lover was Bill MacDowell, a married man with two children who was also the accountant and Company Secretary for Hugh MacRae & Company. The affair had been going on for several years, certainly since 1971, and Andrew's biological father was Bill MacDowell, not Gordon MacRae. However, very few people other than Valerie knew the identity of Renee's lover and even fewer knew that Gordon MacRae wasn't Andrew's father.

Renee had been happy and very excited on the Friday morning because she and Bill were planning to spend time in Perth together. Bill was married with children and it was difficult for them to spend much time together so Renee was particularly looking forward to the weekend. Valerie also told police that Renee had said that Bill MacDowell had been offered a job by a petrochemical company based on

Shetland. Renee had also told her friend that Bill had decided to leave his wife and children and that he had accepted the new job and had already found a four-bedroom house in Shetland in which he planned to live with Renee and Andrew. Renee was expecting a move to Shetland to happen the following weekend (20th/21st November). This surprised Valerie Steventon. She had known about Renee's affair with Bill MacDowell for some time and it had always been her impression that Renee was much more invested in the relationship than Bill. It had never occurred to Valerie that Bill might leave his wife and start a new life with Renee, but that was what her friend told her. Renee was seemed extremely happy at the prospect of starting a new life with Bill.

Renee also told Valerie that she would be very relieved to finally be able to spend time openly with Bill. She had generally not told people the identity of her lover because she was afraid that his wife would find out and that he would be fired from his job with the construction company if Gordon MacRae found out. However, as he had a new job in Shetland, this would no longer be an issue and she was looking forward to finally being able to tell people about the relationship. The trip to Perth was, she told Ms Steventon, a sort of rehearsal for the two living together. Like many people, Ms Steventon wasn't initially too concerned for

Renee's safety. She explained later in a newspaper interview:

> *"Nothing seemed to make sense from the start. When Renee's car was found I genuinely believed it had been set on fire by vandals after she had abandoned it outside Inverness following an argument with Bill MacDowell. I genuinely believed that she had gone on to Perth with Andrew regardless, travelling south by train. On the Monday and Tuesday after she disappeared I even stood on the platform at Inverness expecting her to show up, but as the days went by it was clear to me that something was terribly wrong."*

This slow dawning of the realisation that something was indeed wrong wasn't confined to Valerie Steventon. When the police contacted Renee MacRae's sister Morag a second time, she admitted that she knew that Renee had not really been planning to visit her in Kilmarnock that weekend. Renee had told her that she was planning to spend the weekend with her lover, though Mrs Govans didn't know his identity. Mrs Govans had been aware for some time that Renee was having an affair with a married man. Morag had tried on several occasions to persuade Renee to give up the relationship, but without success. Although they lived apart, the two sisters were still very close and spoke on the telephone every Sunday, but Renee hadn't phoned on Sunday 14th November as arranged. Mrs Govans told the police that, as a result, she too was very worried about her sister's safety.

Police spoke to Gordon MacRae. He provided a convincing alibi for the Friday evening and admitted that he had called Morag Govans on the Saturday, after police told him about the discovery of the burned-out car. She had told him that Renee and Andrew weren't with her but, he explained, he hadn't been too concerned for her safety at that time. He had known for many years that Renee had a lover, though he had no idea of his identity. He had assumed that Renee was most likely with her lover that weekend and surmised, as the police initially had, that her car had been left parked somewhere in Inverness and stolen by joy-riders. As time went on with no word from Renee, Gordon MacRae also became concerned for his wife's well-being

Next, the police spoke with Bill MacDowell. He admitted to having been Renee MacRae's lover for a number of years and agreed that he was Andrew's biological father. He also admitted that he had considered leaving his wife to be with Renee and he had initially agreed to meet Renee and Andrew on that Friday evening so that they could spend the weekend together in Perth. However, he told the police that he had changed his mind at the last moment and had not met with Renee. His wife Rosemary confirmed that he had not left their family home that Friday evening.

Bill MacDowell and Renee MacRae

Photo: Ken MacPherson

MacDowell absolutely denied that he had told Renee that he had found a new a job in Shetland, or that he planned leaving his wife and children and moving there to live with her. However, MacDowell did tell the police one very interesting thing: He mentioned that he and Renee had a system of coded telephone rings, so that Renee could let him know that she was calling without alerting his wife – she would let the phone ring a certain number of times, then hang up and then call again immediately. Twice over the weekend the phone had rung in that particular way, indicating that Renee wanted to talk with him. He hadn't wanted to talk to her and had not answered the telephone.

Despite this piece of evidence, which seemed to suggest strongly that Renee had been alive and well over the weekend, the police were still very concerned. The stain on the rug found in the boot of Renee's BMW had been analyzed and it was found to be human blood of the same type as that of Renee and Andrew. In a press conference, Northern Constabulary said that they had no direct evidence that a crime had been committed, but that they were treating the disappearance of Renee and Andrew as suspicious. Behind the scenes, it was very clear that the police were focusing on a search for bodies, not living people.

The Northern Constabulary investigation was undertaken on a massive scale. It was headed by Detective Superintendent Ian Cameron and, under his direction, one hundred police officers supported by several hundred members of the public and troops from the Kings Own Scottish Borderers from nearby Fort George took part in a search of the area near where the car had been discovered. All police leave was cancelled, personnel from the Scottish Crime Squad in Glasgow were called to Inverness to assist and a BMW specialist was called in to examine the car (he found nothing mechanically wrong with it other than damage caused by the fire). Over five hundred properties in and around Inverness were searched, (including a detailed search in the area close to Renee MacRae's bungalow), and more than five thousand statements were taken. Farmers, shepherds, gamekeepers and trackers were asked to be on the alert for signs of newly disturbed earth and/or digging in the area of the A9.

A sub-aqua team from Stirling was called in to search nearby Loch Moy as well as the Funtack Burn and the River Findhorn, but they failed to find any clues. A helicopter was used to search for possible burial sites and at one point a specially equipped RAF Canberra bomber was tasked to take infra-red surveillance photographs of the area round the A9 in the hope that these might shown the location of freshly turned earth. Ten days after her disappearance, Gordon MacRae told the press that he was "*sick with worry*" and offered a reward for any information about Renee or Andrew. It was rumoured that the police even consulted diviners and psychics in an effort to discover what had happened to the missing pair but none of this activity produced any tangible trace of either of them.

The landscape around Moy over which the search for Renee and Andrew MacRae took place is wild and inhospitable. In November 1976, heavy rain turned many areas into a quagmire.

Photo: Sarah McGuire

At one of a series of press conferences held by Northern Constabulary around one week after the disappearance, Chief Constable Donald Henderson suddenly broke into answers being given by other officers to say: *"We now fear that Mrs Christina MacRae and her three year old son Andrew may be dead because of the expiry of time."*

A poster issued by Northern Constabulary and widely distributed around the Highlands at the time of the disappearance.

Northern Constabulary

When they visited Renee's bungalow in Cradlehall, the police discovered that many of her clothes and possessions and some of Andrew's toys and clothes had been packed into boxes, as if Renee was preparing for a move in the near future. This seemed to support what she had told her friend Valerie Steventon about expecting an imminent move to Shetland to be with Bill MacDowell. However, MacDowell reiterated that did not have a new job and he denied ever telling Renee that he would be leaving his wife or that he and Renee would be moving to Shetland together.

Around two weeks after the disappearance of Renee and Andrew, Bill MacDowell unexpectedly arrived at Northern Constabulary HQ on Old Perth Road on the outskirts of Inverness and asked to talk to detectives involved in the case. Before he could say anything, his wife Rosemary arrived and angrily demanded that he leave. She had been driving past, she explained, when she had seen MacDowell's Volvo estate car in the car park outside. To the amazement of detectives, she burst into the interview room and literally dragged her husband out of the building, telling him to say nothing, accusing police of hounding him unfairly and demanding that they leave him alone.

MacDowell gave only one, brief interview to the press in the aftermath of the disappearance. He admitted being Renee MacRae's lover and the father of Andrew, but denied having any involvement in her disappearance. A short time later, MacDowell was dismissed from Hugh MacRae & Company and he and his wife moved to London.

Police were so desperate for new information that they brought in a hypnotist in order to help witnesses recall as much as possible. Both Gordon MacRae and Valerie Steventon underwent hypnosis sessions, but neither recalled anything new or helpful. Bill MacDowell declined to be hypnotised.

One thing that did come to light as a result of police

investigations was that things weren't quite as rosy as they appeared at Hugh MacRae & Company. Accounts showed that the firm had lost almost half a million pounds in 1976, a massive and unsustainable loss. The company had managed to continue only by an issue of 14,000 of its shares (organised in part by Bill MacDowell) which saw the £1 shares being valued at £8 each. In 1977, Gordon MacRae sold Renee's bungalow in Cradlehall and made a tidy 25% profit on the deal.

In January 1977, two months after the disappearance, Chief Constable Donald Henderson was asked about the case during a presentation to the Police Committee in Inverness. He told the committee that there were four possible explanations for the disappearance:

- Renee had decided to commit suicide and to kill Andrew.

- Renee and Andrew had been involved in some sort of accident which had either disabled or killed them.

- Renee MacRae had decided to leave the area voluntarily with her son but without telling anyone where she was going.

- Renee and Andrew had been murdered and their bodies concealed.

He told the committee that there was no evidence of mental

illness or any inclination towards depression or suicide on the part of Renee MacRae, which had led police to rule out suicide. If there had been an accident, there would have been some trace found of Renee or Andrew by now, so that too was considered very unlikely. The police could not be completely certain that Renee MacRae had not chosen to disappear, but they had found no evidence to suggest this was the case and it was considered very unlikely. He admitted there were "*good reasons*" to believe that the only remaining possibility, murder, was the reason for the disappearance. However, he said: "*As to what happened, where it happened, and how it happened, we have not a clue.*"

Chapter 4: Two quarries and a dead sheep

In terms of hard evidence, the police seemed to have very little to go on. Renee MacRae and Andrew were missing as was their luggage and Andrew's pushchair. The luggage and pushchair were not found in the remains of the burned-out car and had not been located. The only useful evidence in the car was the bloodstain on the rug in the boot. The blood on the rug was of the same type as Renee and Andrew's and the stain was at different times described by the police as *'small'* and *'fairly significant'*. It wasn't sufficiently large to prove conclusively that a murder had been committed, but the clear implication was that either Mrs MacRae or Andrew or both had been placed in the boot of the car while they were dead or injured. Beyond this, there was no hard evidence of what had happened at all.

The only significant information that the police had received was eyewitness testimony. Mrs MacRae had been seen at around five o'clock when she dropped her son Gordon at the offices where her husband worked in Cradlehall Business Park, not far from her bungalow. That was the last confirmed sighting. No-one could be found who had seen Mrs MacRae or her car after that time and before it was found in lay-by 162. However, what appeared to be a potentially significant sighting was provided by two men who had been in a car driving on a narrow farm road towards the A9 at around 19:30 on the evening of 12th November. The road they were on joined the A9 only around fifty metres from the entrance to lay-by 162, where one and a half hours later the burning BMW was found. Approximately 200 metres before joining the A9, they reported seeing a blue hatchback-type car, possibly a Volkswagen Golf or a Volvo 340, parked at the side of the road. They were able to provide police with partial number plate information and they also saw a man who was dragging something that they said looked like a dead sheep up the embankment and through a firebreak which led towards the north edge of Dalmagarry Quarry.

Given that Mrs MacRae had been wearing a sheepskin coat when she was last seen alive and that this sighting was very close to where her car was found, this was felt to be a very important and promising lead. Later, another witness came forward who had been driving on the A9 on the evening of 12th November and remembered seeing a man wheeling a pushchair along the side of the road in the vicinity of Dalmagarry Quarry. Suddenly, the quarry became the focus of a great deal of police attention.

Dalmagarry Quarry had been used as a source for gravel and sand during the construction of new stretches of the A9. It was an open-cast quarry and excavations weren't especially deep, but the quarry was screened from the A9 by an embankment that ran round its perimeter. The quarry had also been used as a place to dump spoil from the most recent improvements to the A9, but by November 1976 it was disused. There was some heavy plant at the quarry which was being used to landscape the area. The quarry was around four hundred meters from lay-by 162 where the burning BMW was found.

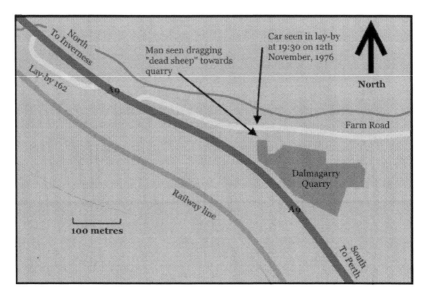

Map showing lay-by 162, Dalmagarry Quarry and the locations where a parked car and a man dragging a '*dead sheep*' towards the quarry were seen on the evening of 12th November.

The quarry was searched soon after the burned-out BMW was found, though no attempt was made at excavation. There were some areas of freshly turned earth, but these were assumed to be part of the on-going landscaping work. The men operating the heavy plant that was being used for this landscaping offered to help by digging, but they were told that this would not be necessary. The police search was organized by Detective Sergeant John Cathcart, and he returned to Dalmagarry Quarry on several occasions, but was unable to find anything significant. In June 1977 he was able to get authorization to hire an excavator to undertake a weekend dig at the quarry. On the Sunday, just as the light was fading and they were about to pack in for the day, the digger removed a section of topsoil and DS Cathcart noted a distinct smell of rotting flesh. He reported this to his superiors but was told that there were no funds available to extend the hire of the excavator or to undertake more digging at the quarry.

The information on the blue car seen in a lay-by close to Dalmagarry Quarry led to police interest in another quarry in the area. Another blue vehicle had been seen on the evening of 12th November in the vicinity of Leanach Quarry. Leanach is actually two, adjacent quarries located on bleak moorland close to Culloden Battlefield, around three miles east of Inverness but less than one mile from Renee

45

MacRae's bungalow. The quarry was excavated during the Victorian period to provide sandstone blocks to build the nearby Culloden railway viaduct and comprises two large, deep, steep-sided pits which have become flooded over the years. Access to the quarry is from a narrow road, the B851 which runs south to join the A9 not far from lay-by 162. This was where the blue car was seen parked on the evening of 12th November.

Police decided that they need to search Leanach Quarry for any sign of Renee or Andrew MacRae. Unfortunately and despite being fenced and gated, the flooded quarries have been used over the years as a convenient spot to dump anything from unwanted cars to garden rubbish and both are filled with tangled masses of junk. Initially, it was hoped that it might be possible to at least partially drain one of the quarries into the other, but it was quickly discovered that they were linked underwater and this was not possible. Two police divers from Northern Constabulary had been killed in a tragic accident a few years before and there was understandable reluctance to send men into the very dangerous waters of the flooded quarry. Instead a submersible camera was lowered into the murky waters in an effort to look for the bodies.

Photo: Rod Allday

One of the pictures captured by the camera was very striking indeed but there was lively debate about just what the small, blurred and indistinct image showed. To some people, the image appeared to show a human face, apparently wrapped inside a plastic bag – some even claimed they could clearly make out eyes and an open mouth. Others were less certain and claimed that the picture showed nothing more than a plastic bag full of rubbish. The Scottish Daily Mail commissioned an artist to produce a version of the image (newspapers were not initially permitted to use the original picture) and the *face from the deep*' became one of the images most associated with the disappearance of Renee MacRae. In November 1977, Northern Constabulary finally released the underwater camera image to the press and as far as many people were concerned, the search for Renee MacRae was over.

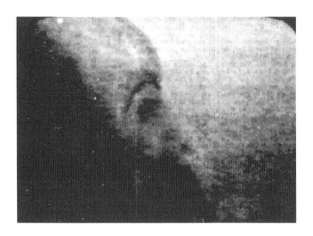

The face from the deep.

Northern Constabulary

When the submersible camera had captured the image, a buoy had been placed in the water to mark the spot. It was decided that it was too dangerous to send a diver from Northern Constabulary into the tangled debris in the quarry and instead a specialist team of divers from the Royal Navy was called to Inverness. In front of a group of representatives from the press, navy divers spent two days in the dark and freezing waters of Leanach Quarry in the winter of 1977. After an agonizing wait they returned to the surface carrying – a plastic bag filled with garden rubbish!

Officially, that was the end of the search in Leanach Quarry, though not all the members of the press were convinced. It was noted, for example, that the divers had simply retrieved a bag of rubbish from close to where the buoy was placed. However, there were those who felt that Leanach was a large quarry and that it would have been very difficult to be certain that the buoy was precisely on the very spot where the image had been captured by the camera. Over the years, hundreds and probably thousands of bags of rubbish and other large items (the divers found a steam lorry from the late 1800s in the depths of the quarry) had been dumped into the quarry and many people felt that a more sustained and detailed underwater search might well have yielded positive results. Despite this, it was decided that it was simply too dangerous to ask divers to remain in the dark waters of the flooded quarries any longer. The search was called off and Leanach Quarry was formally ruled out of the investigation.

As far as many people were concerned, the investigations at both Dalmagarry and Leanach quarries had been abandoned too soon. The sighting of the car and man dragging the *dead sheep* towards Dalmagarry Quarry was seen by some as the most important clue to what had happened to Renee and Andrew. The sighting of what may have been the same car and the striking underwater image from Leanach Quarry convinced others that this should be the focus of the police effort. For different reasons (budget restraints at Dalmagarry and safety at Leanach) neither of these avenues of investigation were pursued and by 1979 the search for the bodies of Renee and Andrew MacRae had been all but abandoned.

The police continued to pursue other lines of enquiry. When Peter Sutcliffe was arrested in 1981 and later charged with what had become known as the Yorkshire Ripper Murders, there was speculation that he might have had some involvement with the disappearance of Renee MacRae. Sutcliffe was a lorry driver who occasionally brought loads to Scotland and who began his series of killings in 1975. However, there was no evidence to associate Sutcliffe with the disappearance of Renee MacRae and no suggestion that he had even been in Scotland in November 1976. Although the case remained formally open, there was still no firm evidence and no good leads about what might have happened to Renee and Andrew on that November night.

In 1980, Gordon MacRae announced that he had obtained a divorce from Renee. Because she had not been officially declared dead, the only way he could extricate himself from the marriage was to apply for divorce on the grounds of separation. This was granted and Gordon then married

Vivienne, the woman he was living with.

In 1991 Bill MacDowell was jailed in England after being found guilty of four separate counts of dishonesty and forgery. It appeared that he had assisted more than one client for whom he worked as an accountant by arranging for them to have a fire which destroyed financial records which might have been of great interest to the Inland Revenue Service. He was charged with doing this for several clients and for sums amounting to almost quarter of a million pounds. None of these things had happened during his time as Company Secretary and accountant for Hugh MacRae & Company and there was no suggestion that these crimes were in any way linked to the disappearance of Renee and Andrew MacRae.

Later, MacDowell blamed the adverse publicity he had received following the MacRae disappearance for his criminal efforts, though he was never able to explain this rationally.

Poor performance in 1976 proved to be only a temporary set-back for Hugh MacRae & Company and the construction firm went on to grow and prosper in the decades that followed. As of 2018, Gordon MacRae and his twin brother Charles were still Directors of the company as was Gordon's second wife, Vivienne.

In 2000 there was brief optimism that the remains of Renee MacRae had been discovered when human bones were found in a small forest in Migdale in Sutherland, around thirty-five miles north of Inverness. However, forensic examination proved these to be the remains of a young man who had gone missing from his home in West Yorkshire in 1997.

Chapter 5: Reverberations

Over the next decades, the question of what might have happened to Renee MacRae and Andrew periodically surfaced in the local and national press, though there was little active police investigation. One of the topics that was repeatedly raised was that of the possible location of the bodies. It was noted, for example, that many stretches of the A9 had been under improvement at the time of the disappearance, and many people wondered whether the bodies might have been concealed under roadworks or parts of the new construction?

There was certainly a great deal of on-going work on the A9 at the time of the disappearance. At one point there was a suspicion that something might have been concealed in the foundations of a new rail bridge on the A9 less than one mile from lay-by 162. A road worker came forward to say that he had found that the foundations for the bridge had been disturbed on the morning after Renee and Andrew disappeared. However, careful perusal of aerial photographs by the police showed conclusively that work on the bridge had not begun until early 1977, making it too late to have been a potential location for the disposal of bodies in November 1976.

It wasn't until early 2004 that there was a notable renewal

of interest in the case when Grampian Television (now STV North) launched a major new documentary series; *Unsolved: Getting Away with Murder*. The series was presented by actor Alex Norton, well-known for his role as DCI Matt Burke in the fictional STV detective series *Taggart*. *Unsolved* investigated some of the most baffling Scottish Murder cases and it began with an episode on the disappearance of Renee and Andrew MacRae, broadcast on 8th January 2004.

One of the segments on the *Unsolved* first episode was an interview with DS John Cathcart, then retired from Northern Constabulary. He told in dramatic terms about the search in Dalmagarry Quarry, described the smell of rotting flesh and said again that he believed that he had been on the point of finding the bodies in June 1977 when his superiors had decided that enough money had been spent on the hire of an excavator. His frustration was still evident almost thirty years later and many people watching the documentary felt the same way – surely this had been a vital clue that had been overlooked in the interests of saving money?

Photo: Dave Conner

Pressure on Northern Constabulary to re-investigate Dalmagarry Quarry increased and later in 2004 Ian Latimer, then Chief Constable, announced a cold case review of the MacRae disappearance which was to be led by Detective Superintendent Gordon Urquhart. The review would include a reinvestigation of Dalmagarry Quarry. The Chief Constable noted:

> *"I feel it is my duty to the family of Renee to find her and her son, return them to her family and do everything in my power to bring the perpetrator of what I feel is a vile and wicked crime to justice. It will be an expensive operation, but finance isn't the issue. Justice is. We will pursue this, no matter the*

cost."

One of the people providing impetus for the re-opening of the case was Chuck Burton, an experienced senior behavioural investigative advisor at the National Centre for Police Excellence in England. Burton spent three days in early 2004 in Inverness looking at the MacRae case using statistical analysis. Burton told the Sunday Herald newspaper: *"We can predict the murderer's age, where he lived, likely relationships, all those sorts of things, including body deposition sites. This tool wasn't available when Renee and Andrew disappeared, so everything is new ground."* After completing this analysis, Burton agreed that Dalmagarry Quarry was the most likely place for the bodies of Renee and Andrew MacRae to have been buried.

On Monday 9th August 2004, a large team descended on Dalmagarry Quarry. Personnel from Northern Constabulary were supported by renowned forensic anthropologist Professor Sue Black from Dundee University and respected forensic archeologist Professor John Hunter from Birmingham University. To many people, it seemed only a matter of time before Dalmagarry Quarry finally gave up its secrets.

NORTHERN CONSTABULARY

MISSING PERSONS

WHERE ARE THEY NOW?

MRS CHRISTINA CATHERINE 'RENEE' MACRAE (36),
5 ft., blonde hair, fresh complexion. Last seen wearing a
¾-length sheepskin coat, maroon slacks, brown
knee-length boots and navy blue chunky cardigan.

ANDREW DAVID MACRAE (3), blonde hair,
son of Mrs Christina Catherine MacRae.

HAVE YOU SEEN THEM?

They were last seen in Inverness about 5 p.m. on Friday, 12th November, 1976. About 9 p.m. that same date Mrs MacRae's
light metallic blue BMW motor car – identical to the photographs shown below and bearing the registration plates in
the photographs – was found burning on the A9 Perth/Inverness road at Dalmagarry, 12 miles south of Inverness. They
have not been seen since.

DID YOU SEE THIS CAR ON 12.11.76?

If you have seen either of these persons – or if you saw Mrs MacRae's car on the A9 road on the evening of Friday,
12th November, 1976 – or if you have any other information – please contact Inverness Police, Tel. No. (0463) 39908 or
any Police Station.

Police Headquarters,
Perth Road, Inverness.

Printed by Highland Printers Ltd., Diriebught Road, Inverness

D. B. HENDERSON
Chief Constable

A poster produced by Northern Constabulary as part of the cold case review and intended to jog memories about the disappearance of Renee and Andrew MacRae.

Northern Constabulary

On August 15th 2004 Bill MacDowell, who had consistently refused to discuss the MacRae case with the press, gave a surprise interview to the Sunday Mail. MacDowell, who had been released from prison following his incarceration on forgery and dishonesty charges and was living in London with his wife Rosemary at the time of the interview, told the newspaper:

> *'I didn't do it. It's all starting up again and it's a nightmare for myself and Rosemary - it keeps following us around. We can't escape it but I didn't do it."*

However, bizarrely, when talking about the new search of Dalmagarry Quarry he also told the reporter:

> *'They should be looking somewhere else.'*

Presumably, MacDowell meant to say that the police should have been looking at a suspect other than himself, but it sounded rather as if he was saying that he knew that the search at Dalmagarry Quarry was pointless. But how could he possibly know that?

More than two thousand trees were felled and around twenty-thousand tons of soil and rock were slowly, painfully moved, sifted and examined in a month-long attempt to find a clue in the quarry. In the event, the exhaustive search of the quarry proved to be just as expensive as the Chief

Constable had anticipated, but produced little in terms of tangible results. It seemed that Bill MacDowell was right – the police should have been looking somewhere else. The final cost of the search is still disputed but it may have cost the taxpayer as much as £250,000. The results? The only material recovered from the site were some items of men's clothing (which were not thought to be related to the MacRae case), two crisp packets and what turned out to be some rabbit bones. It was evident that, wherever Renee and Andrew were, they weren't in Dalmagarry Quarry.

Forensic Anthropologist Professor Sue Black, pictured at the Bloody Scotland International Crime Writing Festival in 2017.

Photo: TimDuncan

Despite this, there were those who continued to claim that Dalmagarry Quarry had been used as the initial burial location for Renee and Andrew. However, supporters of this theory suggested that the murderer had heard about the use of an excavator in June 1977 and had subsequently dug up the bodies and re-buried them elsewhere. When asked about this, Professor Sue Black admitted that she couldn't rule out this possibility though neither she nor anyone else was able to produce evidence to support this idea.

The cold case review continued and in September 2006, Northern Constabulary announced that the review and the excavations at Dalmagarry Quarry had "*closed an evidential gap*" and that they had submitted a new report to the procurator fiscal. It was known that the report named a suspect, but this person was not publically identified. In Scotland, a report is provided by the police to the office of the procurator fiscal who then decides if there is sufficient evidence to take the case to trial. In December 2006 the Crown Office released the following announcement:

> *"Following full and careful consideration of the detailed review report submitted in September 2006 by Northern Constabulary, Crown counsel has concluded that there is insufficient evidence for criminal proceedings against any person at this time. As with all major unsolved investigations, the*

case will remain open. Should any further evidence come to light in this long-running inquiry it will be carefully considered by Northern Constabulary and the procurator fiscal."

There was renewed interest in this case after the cold case review and many potential sites where the bodies might have been buried were discussed. Several of these were publicized by Brian MacGregor, a local man who lives in Bogbain Farm, beside the A9 and around six miles north of lay-by 162. Mr MacGregor is a former garage owner and a voluble and angry man who has little enthusiasm for the work of Northern Constabulary. Motorists driving south on the A9 are occasionally entertained and enlightened by the large signs he sometimes places in the fields next to the A9, often ranting about the activities (or lack of activity) of Northern Constabulary. Bogbain Farm houses a modest agricultural heritage and visitor centre and on occasion this public venue has also been used to display material relating to the disappearance of Renee MacRae.

There is no doubting that Mr MacGregor's enthusiasm and energy have generated results (it was his placement of an advertisement asking for information more than twenty years after the disappearance that led to road workers coming forward with potential locations on the A9), but so far nothing that he has done has provided any concrete evidence about what may have happened to Renee and Andrew. In 2005 Mr MacGregor paid for a metal detector scan of a section of road around one mile north of lay-by 162. The scan identified something metallic seemingly buried under the road – Mr MacGregor believes this may be Andrew's pushchair. To date, no excavations have been undertaken to check what lies buried beneath the road but Northern Constabulary (now part of Police Scotland) have put in place protocols to ensure that anything found during on-going improvement work on the road will be brought to their attention.

Mr MacGregor's advertisements also produced one other witness who claimed to have seen Renee's MacRae's car on the night that she disappeared. In 2006, MacGregor was contacted by Jock Campbell, a local man who on 12th November 1976 had been clear-felling trees adjacent to the A9, approximately three miles south of Inverness and nine miles north of lay-by 162. As he was leaving the site sometime after four o'clock he claims that he saw Renee MacRae's car being driven south on the A9. He recognised the car because he had been employed to undertake landscaping work at several MacRae housing developments and he had seen the car before. His attention was drawn to the car because it was driving so slowly on what is a very long straight – he estimated that it was doing no more than forty miles an hour and was being driven by a man. Mr Campbell wasn't sure about the time, though he described it as "*gloaming*" (after sunset but before full dark). This means that it was most probably around four thirty and certainly no later than four-forty five.

Mr Campbell is very certain about his sighting but the problem is that this doesn't fit with what we know about Renee MacRae's movements on that day: she dropped Gordon off at her husband's office after darkness had fallen at approximately five o'clock in her car, so it's difficult to see how the same car could have been seen heading south on the A9 driven by someone else fifteen or thirty minutes before.

This tends to highlight the problems of witnesses who come forward many years after the event. Human memory is known to be a malleable and a fallible thing and memories of long-ago events may be quite different to what actually happened. Although these witnesses may genuinely believe what they say to be true, it is unwise to place too much weight on memories of events which have taken place many years before. However, Mr MacGregor has used this and other evidence to suggest that the solution to the disappearance of Renee and Andrew may be attributable to a complex conspiracy involving professional hit-men, the MacRae family and the Freemasons. While it may be entertaining, there is little about this theory to commend it to anyone looking for a rational and credible solution to this mystery.

Other suggestions about what might have happened to Renee and Andrew MacRae have been provided by a number of unlikely people including diviners and psychics over the years. In the most recent example, in September 2016 the Scottish Daily Express ran an extended piece covering claims by psychic investigators Archibald Lawrie and Frances Ryan. Mr Lawrie is the President of the Edinburgh Society for Psychical Research and Ms Ryan is one of Scotland's best-known mediums. They claimed that Ms Ryan had a vision where she saw Renee MacRae driving on the B1954 and being pursued by another car before being forced off the road, killed and buried in a clearing in a wooded area close to the Allt na Loinne Mor burn. The spot they claim is the burial site is close to what used to be the Moy Halt railway station and around one mile from lay-by 162. The psychic investigators also visited the lay-by and Ms Ryan had a vision of the BMW being dumped there by two men, *"one well-dressed with an open necked shirt and hair brushed to the back of his head and the other sitting in another car smoking."*

Like many suggestions provided by psychics and others who claim to use paranormal powers, the information provided is maddeningly incomplete. The visions in this example provide fairly detailed descriptions of the two men dumping the BMW for example (though not sufficiently detailed to identify any specific individual), but do not provide truly useful information such as the make, colour or registration number of the second car. Whether you believe these accounts provide helpful information that might contribute towards the solution of this case rather depends on whether or not you believe that psychic investigators have access to special information. It's certainly notable that none of the tips gleaned from paranormal sources have yielded any tangible evidence so far.

Other people have claimed to know what happened to Renee and Andrew, though they all seem to give a different account of both the murder and to identify different places where the bodies are buried. For example, in 2004, Mr Piercy Philip used divining rods to pinpoint what he said was the precise location in Dalmagarry Quarry where the bodies were buried, an area which for some reason was not included in the dig during the summer of that year. An anonymous letter to a local newspaper in the early 2000s claimed that a group of five people, including a police officer, had conspired to abduct and murder Renee MacRae. The letter also claimed that Andrew was still alive and living abroad but it failed to provide any evidence to support these claims. There have been many such statements, but none have provided a plausible and provable solution to the mystery.

Chapter 6: What happened to Renee and Andrew McRae?

Just as Northern Constabulary Chief Constable Donald Henderson said back in January 1977, there are just four possible options in the case of the disappearance of Renee and Andrew MacRae:

- Renee MacRae committed suicide and killed Andrew.

- There was an accident which led to the deaths of both Renee and Andrew.

- Renee MacRae left Inverness for a new life and a new identity, taking Andrew with her.

- Renee and Andrew MacRae were murdered and their bodies concealed.

Let's take these in order. First of all, there is no evidence that Renee MacRae was suicidal or even depressed in November 1976. On the contrary, she was said to have been very happy at the prospect of moving to Shetland with Bill MacDowell. However, if she had decided to kill herself without anyone knowing, just how could this have worked? She would have to have driven her car to lay-by 162, set it on fire and then, presumably walked off into the wilderness with Andrew to die of exposure, stopping only to take her luggage and Andrew's pushchair with her. This didn't sound likely in 1976 and it sounds even less so now – surely, if Renee and Andrew's bodies were somewhere in the open, in the vicinity of lay-by 162, they would have been discovered by now? I think we can reasonably rule out suicide as a possibility in this case.

What about an accident? Let's suppose that Renee was driving on the A9 when suddenly she became aware that her car was on fire. She pulled into the first available lay-by, which happened to be 162. Then, presumably partially incapacitated by fumes, she stumbled off with Andrew in her arms and died of exposure. While carrying her luggage and his pushchair. This doesn't sound very likely either, does it? And, if she did find herself stranded beside a burning car, surely she would have been more likely to stay by the A9 to await help. And, just as in the suicide scenario, the bodies couldn't have ended up too far from lay-by 162, so surely they would have been found by now? Just like suicide, I think we can reasonably rule out an accident in this case.

What then of the possibility that Renee MacRae chose to disappear? This has seriously been suggested as a solution by some people - you'll note for example that the second poster issued by Northern Constabulary, during the cold case review in 2004, appealed for witnesses who might have seen Renee MacRae or Andrew after 12th November 1976.

To assume a new identity and a new life requires first money and second contact with the kind of people who can forge identity papers. Renee MacRae had very little money of her own. Although her estranged husband provided generously for her after they split, she simply didn't have her own source of income. She had some jewellery, but most of this was found at her home in Cradlehall. There is no evidence at all that Renee had contact with the kind of people who might have provided her with forged identity documents. If she planned to assume a new identity, she could only have done this the help of someone else. However, her closest friends were adamant that in late 1976, the only man in her life was Bill MacDowell, with whom she seemed completely besotted.

If we add to this the fact that there have been no sightings of Renee MacRae since 12th November 1976, and only one person (Bill MacDowell) has claimed that she tried to contact him after that date, then, although it's not completely impossible, the idea that Renee MacRae chose to disappear and assume a new identity seems so unlikely that I think it can be safely discarded as a theory.

Which leaves us with the last option: that someone murdered Renee and Andrew MacRae. Just as it was in January 1977, this remains the most likely option to account for the disappearance. However, of the murders themselves, when and where and how they were committed, I don't think we will ever know for certain unless one day the bodies of Renee and Andrew are found.

But, I think there are some obvious inferences that we can draw. First let's consider where were the bodies might have been disposed of? I can't tell you with certainty where they were buried, but I am confident that I can tell you where they weren't buried, and that's anywhere in the vicinity of lay-by 162 on the A9. Let's try to put ourselves inside the head of a murderer for a moment, and see if I can explain why I believe that.

I think we can assume that Renee MacRae's BMW was burned for a very specific reason. After all, if you simply wanted to dump a car somewhere it wouldn't be found quickly, the best place would be with lots of other cars – in a station or airport car-park, for example. Do that, and you can assume it will be days or perhaps even weeks before anyone realises that the car is dumped. Setting fire to it by the side of a major road at night means that it is going to be found by the police very quickly, so there must be a good reason for taking this risk. The obvious conclusion is that there was some forensic evidence in the car, blood perhaps or maybe the murderer, who must have driven the car, wanted to ensure that there were no fingerprints, or fibres or hairs that could give him away.

Photo: Richard Hopkins

If you are going to burn a vehicle, you really need somewhere out of sight of a main road – you don't want someone to drive past just as you're setting the car alight. If it's somewhere as desolate as the Highlands you are also going to need the assistance of a confederate with another car. Once you have set the BMW alight, you want to get out of the area as quickly as possible, and you can't risk trying to hitch-hike or catch a bus and there is nowhere close to which you can walk. You need another car standing by to take you away. But, you don't want any passing vehicle to see your getaway car (which can presumably be traced to you or your confederate) along with the car you're about to burn.

In that sense, lay-by 162 was pretty nearly perfect and suggests that the person who left the car there had thought this through in advance and that they knew the area. It is possible to drive from Inverness to the part of the A9 on which the lay-by is located by using quiet back roads. The B9154 joins the A9 less than two hundred metres from lay-by 162, so it would only be necessary to drive for a very short distance on this busy road. Once you have pulled both cars into the lay-by, no passing vehicles could see you because of the embankment (and that's not true of virtually any other lay-by on the Perth-Inverness stretch of the A9). Because it was dark, you could also ensure that there were no approaching vehicles by looking for headlights before you set fire to the BMW and left the lay-by in the getaway car.

All of this suggests a high degree of intelligence and forward planning in terms of getting rid of the BMW. Now let's consider the bodies. The murderer knows that the burning car is going to be spotted and will attract the attention of the police. However, as long as the bodies aren't found, it's going to be very difficult for the police to turn this into a murder investigation. The murderer must accept that the car is going to be found but must do everything possible to ensure that the bodies aren't found.

Police will quickly descend on the burning car and, once

they realise that Renee and Andrew are missing, they will begin to search in the immediate area because, at that point, they can't be sure that the occupants of the BMW haven't just wandered off and got lost. So, where is the murderer going to hide the bodies? As far from the burning BMW as possible! To suggest that the murderer dumped the bodies in Dalmagarry Quarry and then set light to the BMW four hundred metres away is just plain silly unless you think the murderer is an idiot. And I don't think that the evidence suggests that he is.

In this case, I am certain that the man seen dragging the dead sheep is a false lead that had nothing to do with Renee or Andrew MacRae or the burning BMW. If we think about it for a moment, if this sighting really was the murderer dragging Renee MacRae's body towards Dalmagarry Quarry, this would mean that he must have driven out to Dalmagarry Quarry in his own car, buried the bodies and then driven back to wherever the BMW was stored and then driven it back to a spot right beside where the bodies were buried. This just doesn't make any kind of logical sense at all – by doing this the murderer would have been drawing the police to the very place where the bodies were buried. I don't know what the witnesses saw that night, perhaps it really was a man dragging a dead sheep towards the quarry, but I certainly don't think it had any bearing on the disappearance of Renee and Andrew MacRae.

Likewise the man apparently seen wheeling a pushchair along the side of the A9. How could this possibly have been anything to do with Renee MacRae? If the bodies were disposed of somewhere, surely the luggage and pushchair would have been too (though I have never understood why the murderer didn't just leave both in the BMW). I cannot imagine any scenario where someone who had just killed a young child would then allow themselves to be seen wheeling a pushchair along the side of a busy road in the dark – something that was almost certain to be remembered by any passing motorist.

For the same reasons that I feel Dalmagarry Quarry is an unlikely place to dispose of the bodies, I also think that it's very unlikely that they were buried in nearby roadworks or construction work on the A9. This would have been much too close to where the car was found and it would not be secure until concreting or the laying of tarmac was complete, which might take several days – time in which the police might have found the bodies.

If we credit the murderer with any intelligence at all, I think that the only logical inference is that the bodies were not buried in the immediate vicinity of lay-by 162. There was a gap of four hours between when Renee MacRae was last seen and when the burning BMW was discovered. That would have provided ample time for the murders to be committed and for the bodies to be taken somewhere for disposal before driving the BMW to lay-by 162.

If we can continue to consider things from the point of view of the murderer, let's think about the disposal of the bodies logically. It's the evening of Friday, 12th November. You must dispose of two bodies as quickly as possible. Outside it's completely dark. Unless you have access to a large and private area of land, burying the bodies is probably out of the question. It's dark and you will need some sort of illumination while you move the bodies and dig a grave. This will make you visible from a great distance and may attract unwelcome attention. Then there is the fact that any newly dug grave will likely be obvious to a searcher and vulnerable to discovery by wild animals or passing dogs. Overall, burial is not a good option.

Disposing of the bodies in deep water is a much better idea, but only if you have a boat – lochs and the sea are simply much too shallow at their margins to provide sufficient depth of water for safe disposal. The only alternative might be a very steep-sided body of water where it would be possible to throw in the bodies, luggage and pushchair from the side and know that they would land in deep water. In short, a place very like Leanach Quarry, the only steep-sided body of deep water anywhere in the vicinity of

Inverness and only a couple of miles from the east side of the city. It has always seemed to me that Leanach Quarry is a much more likely spot for the disposal of the bodies of Renee and Andrew MacRae than Dalmagarry Quarry. It is a great pity that more effort wasn't put into searching the quarry in 1977, though the safety concerns were entirely understandable. Deep, cold water filled with debris and rubbish is one of the most hazardous environments in which to dive, so the reluctance of the police to keep men in the water makes perfect sense.

If we accept that Renee and Andrew MacRae were murdered and that their bodies were disposed of, possibly in Leanach quarry but certainly not anywhere in the vicinity of lay-by 162, this brings us to the final and possibly the most important question of all: who murdered them?

There is no evidence to suggest that this was a random killing. The way in which the car was disposed of and the fact that the bodies weren't found despite an intensive and wide-ranging search suggest calm and considered planning and not, for example, a panicked response to an accidental killing during a robbery gone wrong. I believe that we are looking here for someone who had a specific motive to kill Renee MacRae and, unless there is another person involved that we know nothing about, there are really only two possible suspects.

One of the two is Renee's estranged husband Gordon MacRae, who some people have suggested is a viable suspect. I don't agree, for a number of reasons. The motive most often suggested is that Hugh MacRae & Company was losing money in 1976, and that therefore Gordon MacRae could not afford a costly divorce. Instead, he decided to have his wife killed. First of all, there is no evidence that Renee MacRae was seeking a divorce from her estranged husband at the time she went missing. She seemed entirely content with an arrangement that provided her with a pleasant home, a comfortable lifestyle and the ability to spend time with her lover whenever he was available. Gordon MacRae and Renee may have been separated and by November 1976 both had other partners, but no-one has produced any evidence that their relationship with each other was anything but good.

In terms of money, Gordon MacRae was independently wealthy and it is doubtful that any divorce settlement, no matter how severe, could have changed that. The MacRae family too had control of a great deal of wealth and it seems very unlikely that money alone would have been a sufficient motive for Gordon MacRae to have had his wife murdered. Overall, I do not believe that Gordon MacRae arranged for the murder of his wife and Andrew and I have yet to see any convincing evidence to support this theory.

The only other suspect in this case is Bill MacDowell. It has been suggested that Bill was considerably less engaged with their relationship than Renee MacRae was, and that he was perhaps looking for a way to end it, though clearly his being Andrew's biological father would have made this very complicated. There is also the consideration that, if the fact of MacDowell's relationship with Renee had become public, keeping his position as Company Secretary and accountant at Hugh MacRae & Company would likely have become impossible and his marriage to Rosemary might also have been at risk.

The story that Renee told friends about Bill intending to leave his wife and having found a job in Shetland and a four-bedroomed house in which he intended to live with her and Andrew also suggests a basic disconnect in the relationship. It appears that Renee really believed this to be true – the fact that she had started packing and there was no-where else that she could have been moving to confirms this. Unless Renee MacRae invented this story herself (and that doesn't really make any sense) this could only have originated with Bill MacDowell and it was clearly a lie, perhaps designed to buy time from an increasingly impatient Renee. This suggests that, in November 1976, Bill MacDowell and Renee MacRae were headed for a very uncomfortable confrontation when Bill finally admitted that he wasn't planning to leave his wife and there wasn't a job waiting for him in Shetland or a house for them to live in.

Then there is the question of what happened on that Friday night. When Renee MacRae met Valerie Steventon for coffee that morning, she was confident that she was going to be spending the weekend in Perth with Bill MacDowell. When she dropped Gordon at her husband's office at five o'clock, she told him she was going to spend the weekend with her sister in Kilmarnock, a cover story for the trip to Perth. So, at five o'clock on that Friday evening, it seems certain that Renee still believed that she was going to Perth with Bill MacDowell. But MacDowell told police that he had changed his mind and that he had decided not to go. Where had they arranged to meet? What happened when, according to MacDowell's version, Renee must have turned up at the rendezvous and discovered he wasn't there? Did she try to contact him? Did she go to his house? Surely, when he failed to turn up, she must have made some attempt to contact him?

None of these questions have ever been satisfactorily answered and it is very easy to envisage a situation where Renee went to MacDowell and confronted him, only to discover that the move to Shetland was a fantasy. Perhaps she threatened to reveal details of their affair to her husband and Bill's wife? Perhaps the confrontation became

79

angry and then violent? Perhaps it even ended with Renee's accidental death? Of course, this is nothing more than surmise which is unsupported by evidence, but it does tie-in with one odd thing that Bill MacDowell told the police. In early interviews, MacDowell explained that Renee had tried to call him twice over the weekend when she went missing on the Friday evening, using her coded telephone rings. This was in the early days of the enquiry when the police wondered whether Renee MacRae might have run off and it strongly supported the notion that she was still alive and well.

However, the bloodstained rug found in the boot of the BMW suggests that whatever happened to Renee MacRae and Andrew had already happened by 9:00 pm on the Friday night. No-one else knew about the system of coded rings so, when Bill MacDowell says that Renee MacRae tried to call him after Friday 12th November, that cannot be true unless the caller was Renee. If Renee really was killed on the Friday evening, then MacDowell must be lying.

The only possible reason for such a lie is to persuade the police that Renee was still alive. The only person who would have had a reason to tell such a lie would be someone who knew that she was actually dead but wanted to deflect the police enquiry. In that early stage of the enquiry, the only person who could have known that Renee was dead was her murderer or a person who had helped to dispose of the bodies.

Another question that has never been answered regards Bill's sudden decision to go to Northern Constabulary HQ in the early days of the enquiry. Just what did he want to say to detectives? We'll never know because his wife dragged him out before he had a chance to speak. There is also other, circumstantial evidence that points towards Bill MacDowell. One of the reasons that police used the underwater camera in Leanach Quarry was that a blue car had been seen on the evening of 12th November in the vicinity of the quarry. Bill MacDowell owned a blue Volvo estate at the time. If a person wanted to drive from Bill MacDowell's home outside Inverness towards the A9 while using only back roads, the most direct route would involve driving first on the B9006 and then branching off onto the B851 before taking un-named back roads towards the B9154, which joins the A9 a very short distance from lay-by 162. This route would take you past the entrance to Leanach Quarry off the B851.

The B851, not far from Leanach Quarry

David Johnston

Because of his later convictions and imprisonment for fraud, we know that Bill MacDowell is capable of gross dishonesty. This makes it difficult to take his protestations of innocence entirely seriously. It is a terrible thing to accuse a man of murder, and worse still to accuse a man of murdering his own three year old son, but that is certainly where the evidence seems to point in this case. There are many people who feel that Bill MacDowell knows where the bodies of Renee and Andrew MacRae are and who believe that when he said in 2004 about the police search of Dalmagarry Quarry *'they should be looking somewhere else'*, that he was making a simple, Freudian slip. It is also widely believed that, when Northern Constabulary submitted a report to the procurator fiscal about this case in 2006, Bill MacDowell was the named suspect, though this was never officially confirmed.

Can we be certain that Renee and Andrew MacRae were murdered on the evening of Friday 12th November 1976? The answer is that we can't be one hundred percent certain, though what little evidence we have overwhelmingly indicates that is what happened. Do we know where their bodies were dumped? For reasons explained in the text, I am confident that the bodies were not buried in Dalmagarry Quarry nor buried under roadworks on the A9 close to lay-by 162. I think it is much more likely that they were disposed of somewhere further from where the car was found and I believe that Leanach Quarry is a very likely location.

In terms of the murderer, only one person has a viable, known motive. That person has acted oddly on at least two occasions in ways that suggest that they know more than they have admitted about the case. That person is known to be willing to act dishonestly and has an alibi provided only by his wife, something that police officers are generally very dubious about. It may never be proved in a court of law, but I believe that person murdered Renee and Andrew MacRae and concealed their bodies somewhere in the vicinity of Inverness.

Conclusion

I cannot imagine how much pain and anguish the disappearance of Renee and Andrew MacRae must have caused (and continues to cause) for her family and friends. It is horrible when someone close dies, but at least in that case the grieving process can begin. When someone simply disappears, there is always hope, no matter how illogical and tenuous that may be, that they will one day return safe and well. Because of that, it must be very, very difficult to come to terms with the idea that they may be dead and to begin to deal with that.

I also cannot imagine how frustrating it must be for police officers involved in a case such as this. Many of the investigating officers in the Renee MacRae case clearly have strong opinions on the fact that murders have been committed and on the identity of the murderer. However, the failure to locate the bodies and a lack of direct evidence means that the case will probably never come to trial.

Bill MacDowell must also live with the suspicion that he is a brutal double murderer. Almost every newspaper article about this case refers to him as *"Bill MacDowell, the main suspect in the Renee MacRae case."* If he is innocent, this is a terrible burden for him to live under and the lack of a trial continues to deny him the opportunity to clear his name.

If the bodies are ever located, this may provide some measure of closure for Renee and Andrew's friends and family, but it is difficult to see how this could lead to a prosecution unless the murderer was been foolish enough to leave clues to his identity with the bodies. That seems very unlikely.

The only other hope is that a new witness may come forward with vital information that will finally provide a solution to this case. In 2016, on the fortieth anniversary of Renee and Andrew's disappearance, her family issued a heartfelt and moving statement to the press:

> *"Forty years have passed since the disappearance of Renee and Andrew and as a family we remain collectively heartbroken to have lost a much loved and cherished mother, sister, brother and friend to many. We cannot give up hope that somebody holds information which could help lead us to the answers as to what happened to our beloved Renee and Andrew.*
>
> *Our message is it is never too late. We are confident these answers will come from the local community and as a family we urge that person to come forward - until such time the person who caused harm to Renee and Andrew will continue to escape*

justice and we will be without closure."

More than forty years ago, Renee MacRae drove off into the darkness of a cold November night in Inverness. She was excited and looking forward to spending time with the man she loved. Instead, it seems certain that she and her young son met with a cruel and unknown fate. The echoes from that evil act still resonate throughout the Highlands.

Nothing can bring back Renee or Andrew and sadly, although this case remains officially open, I think it is possible that we may never know precisely what happened to them. All we can hope is that one day, someone, somewhere may find their remains so that at least their families can finally lay them to rest.

Photo: Richard Webb

I hope you enjoyed reading this book. If you did, please take a moment to leave me a review on Amazon. Your opinion matters and positive reviews help me greatly. Thank you.

I welcome feedback from readers. If you have comments on this book or ideas for other books in the Murder World series, please send me an email at: stevemac357@gmail.com.

About the Author

Steve is a Scot who writes non-fiction on a range of topics including true crime and the paranormal. He has been interested in crime writing since he read his first true crime book at the local library in 1971, when everyone thought he was studying for his homework. Now he doesn't have to do it in secret anymore and reads a range of work by various crime writers.

He is married with two grown-up children and currently lives in Andalucía in Spain.

Other Murder World: Scotland books

If you enjoyed this book, you may also be interested in these other Murder World: Scotland Books which are available on Amazon:

The Butler's Story: The extraordinary life and crimes of Archibald Thomson Hall

Archibald Thompson Hall was a complicated man. A bisexual born in the working-class back streets of Glasgow, he craved culture and the finer things in life. Sadly, his life hadn't equipped him with the means to obtain these so he stole them instead. He worked as a burglar, thief and con-man for many years before stumbling on a role that suited him well – he became a butler and transformed himself into the urbane, charming and imperturbable gentleman's gentleman Roy Fontaine.

Working as a butler certainly gave him opportunities to steal and embezzle from his employers, but it also led him to face arrest, conviction and prison on more than one occasion (though he became the first person to escape from one of Britain's first high-security prisons). It wasn't until 1977, when he was fifty-three, that he finally discovered his true vocation as a murderer. He committed his first murder in November 1977 and by January the following year he had killed five people and would almost certainly have gone on to kill many more if he hadn't been caught.

This is the true story of a charming, charismatic, intelligent, entertaining, cold, ruthless and merciless killer and one of the most dangerous men in the annals of Scottish crime.

A killing at kinky cottage: The murder of Max Garvie

The Swinging sixties eventually reached even the tranquil Howe O' the Mearns in the North-East of Scotland. Millionaire farmer Max Garvie and his glamorous wife Sheila became so well-known for their nudist and sex parties that their farmhouse became known locally as *'kinky cottage.'*

However, beneath the swinging exterior, all was not well in the marriage of Max and Sheila. Max was easily bored and constantly sought new sexual adventures and partners. Sheila was interested in a more stable and lasting relationship, but not with Max.

Then, one evening in May 1968, the peace and quiet of this tranquil farming community was ripped apart by a shotgun blast. It seemed that Sheila had finally found a permanent way to solve her marital problems. But was it really that simple?

Death in a cold town: The Arlene Fraser case

One Morning in April 1998, attractive mother and housewife Arlene Fraser called her children's school in the town of Elgin on the Moray coast of Scotland. She wanted to know what time her son would be returning from a school trip? That was the last time that anyone had contact with Arlene.

When a friend arrived at her house two hours later, she found no sign of Arlene and no-one has seen her since.

The search for Arlene Fraser became one of the biggest and longest running missing person cases ever seen in Scotland but no clue was found to indicate what had happened to her. Was she abducted and murdered on the instructions of Nat, her estranged husband as the police claimed? Did she run away to a new life, leaving her children, her home and her friends behind? Was she somehow involved in smuggling?

This book provides a detailed look at Arlene Fraser's disappearance, the trials and the legal maneuvering and appeals which followed. It also analyses the main theories of what may have happened to Arlene to assess which is the most likely.

The Face of Bible John: The search for a Scottish serial killer

Just like any other country, Scotland has its share of unsolved crimes. However, few have proved to be as enduringly fascinating as the story of the man who became known as Bible John and who killed three women in Glasgow in the late 1960s.

This murderer picked up each of his three victims at the popular Barrowland Ballroom in the east of the city centre. All three were mothers, all had been menstruating at the time of their death, all were beaten and strangled and all were found close to their own homes.

The murderer made no attempt to conceal or disguise himself and was seen by a number of witnesses at the ballroom and outside - one witness actually shared a taxi with the killer and one of his victims. Through discussions with these witnesses, a well-known artist working on behalf of the police produced a striking portrait of a man with red hair and blue/grey eyes and wearing a cold, rather supercilious expression. This portrait was widely publicized and became known as the face of Bible John.

The murderer frequented a busy public place and was seen with all his victims by a number of witnesses who got a good look at him. By the time of the third murder, there had been massive publicity and people were on their guard and actually looking for a potential killer. How did this person manage to kill three times and yet still escape detection despite having his likeness on the front page of every major Scottish newspaper? Having killed three times, why did he stop? Did he stop at all or did he just become more adept at hiding his crimes? Perhaps most importantly of all, did Bible John really exist at all or was he nothing more than an urban myth?

Printed in Great Britain
by Amazon

53063836R00057